CROSSINGS

A MEMOIR IN VERSE

Gerry Sloan

Photography by Rick Squires

Rollston Press

Crossings
by Gerry Sloan

Copyright © 2017 Gerry Sloan
Photographs © 2017 Rick Squires

ISBN-13: 978-0-9970748-5-7
ISBN-10: 0-9970748-5-X

Also by Gerry Sloan:

Paper Lanterns, Half Acre Press, 2011

Rollston Press
330 N. Rollston Avenue
Fayetteville, Arkansas 72701

For my grandchildren: Soraya, Luciya, Brendan, Jinhao, and Miles.

Acknowledgements: I would like to thank John Rule, Dick Bennett, and Rick Squires for helpful advice on earlier versions of these poems; also Wanna Zhang for photo editing, and Gary Coover for his trust and boundless patience.

TABLE OF CONTENTS

Preface

Born of the rugged scrappy wildernesses of eastern Oklahoma's Ouachita Mountains and the Ozarks of Northwestern Arkansas, these poems of Gerry Sloan's evoke an era of a time and place gone by the wayside in today's rush toward instant electronic gratification. There is a starkness in some of the stories, yet there is also warmth and family and a wealth of personal memories brought forward into the present day from the struggles of yesteryear.

It is our distinct pleasure to be able to bring these minimalist "odes" to you and to share Gerry's poetic stories of his upbringing in a part of the great American Midwest relatively unknown to many. Within this collection of mosaics are wonderful tales of his father, love, family, fishhooks, Methodists, BB-guns, trombones and Choctaws.

As counterpoint to the poetry, Gerry has collaborated with his friend, Rick Squires, to provide a visual gallery not meant to illustrate but rather create a corresponding visual evocation of "a past / that keeps seeding and receding." We hope you enjoy the results.

Gary R. Coover, Managing Editor/Publisher
Rollston Press

I. Prologue: Once Upon A Time In Arkansas

It's very difficult to keep the line between the past and present. Do you know what I mean? It's awfully difficult.

– Little Edie Beale
(*Grey Gardens*, directed by the Maysles brothers)

ETERNITY AS A CONTACT SPORT

In the early August heat, a chickadee
is so thirsty it settles for a drink
in the drip-pan of my begonias,
so close to my perch on the upper deck
I could reach out and touch its airy desperation.

Birds of a feather, we could measure together
the sun's intense displeasure, guess if we would
its origin, some wormhole in the fabric
of space and time where the myriad dead
have come to mingle with those of us yet living.

ANCESTRAL ODE
(Eliza Slone, 1837–1885)

Rarely philosophical, it occurred
to her one day while hoeing onions,
her husband buried in the yard:
"Big fish keep eatin' the little 'uns;
it's the only law you can count on."

Time has little meaning by itself.
We swim in it the way fish
swim in the sea,
cognizant momentarily
of a name engraved on a headstone.

GRANDFATHER OF MY GRANDFATHER

My grandfather and his brothers
were not large men but could clear out
any bar in Crawford County,
according to family legend,
which might be redneck meanness

were it not retaliation for
the murder of their grandfather
by his neighbors during the Civil War,
their perverse version of vengeance
two generations later.

ONCE UPON A TIME IN ARKANSAS

the forest yielded its bounty
as seasons rolled along, dry
kindling ushering flame
to the chopped firewood.
In summer too hot to sleep.

In winter the quilt so heavy
your toes ached if you slept
on your back, waking to splash
your face from the frozen basin,
toweled before starting the chores.

STILL LIFE
(for John Rule)

Some of us living in Arkansas still
can recall a mule-powered
sorghum mill.
And some remember how to tap
a maple tree, distilling the sap

in a cast-iron blackened kettle.
Some also know about hominy,
how to soften dried corn with lye,
or practice the ancient alchemy
of changing grain into alcohol.

THE LORD'S WORK
(after Vance Randolph)

The circuit rider came before sunset,
hoping for a meal. "Brother (So-and-So),
that's a nice stand of corn you and the Lord
have grown." Thank you. (Pause.) "And that's
a nice row of beans you and the Lord planted."

Thanks. (Longer pause.) "And that's a fine bed
of potatoes you and the Lord made over there."
Finally exasperated, the farmer then replied,
"Preacher, you should of seen this spread
when the Lord was working it alone."

CRY OF THE BEAR

Old man Gaskins lived in a cabin
north of Eureka Springs. His lifelong
passion was hunting bears, of which he
killed more than 200 by his reckoning,
which occupies most of his memoirs.

"If pressed they will fight to the end,"
he said. "A bear never hollers till he gets
a death wound, and then he cries 'Oh Lord.'
At least it sounds like that; I could always
tell when he was done for by that cry."

OSAGE ORANGE
(for Rick Squires)

Does the spider know its gossamer web

mimics the whorled rings of your wood,

the former evanescent as air, the latter

so hard that pioneers used you

for making fence-posts? Does anyone notice

that your apparent disproportion

reflects The Golden Mean, observed once

by the ancients, the laws of symmetry

highly overrated? Can anybody guess

the secrets etched into your grain?

WHICH FINGER?

They are mostly gone, men who would give
the one-fingered wave on the backroads,
ceding your half of the right-of-way
as they chugged along in first gear,
never lifting a hand from the wheel.

The new generation would as likely
give you the middle finger, if they
bothered to acknowledge at all,
cruising along the county roads
that are mostly now paved over.

ANCESTRY.COM

My Aunt Nellie claimed to have courted
in a horse-drawn buggy and have seen
men land on the moon, courted under
the giant oak at Newberry Cemetery,
the tree where we would picnic later

on Decoration Day, an amazing array
of food spread sumptuously on tables
covered with checkered cloths, dishes
beyond description, as we kids played
hide-and-seek among the tombstones.

II. Leaving Heavener

The moon will eclipse
Any words on your lips

– Rick Squires

HILL CEMETERY

More and more unsteady at 89,
my mother refuses to use a cane
from pride or vanity, grips my arm
as I once gripped her hand at age 3
on this guided tour of the cemetery,

reciting names on the headstones
as if they had lived only yesterday,
sharing gossipy tidbits post-mortem
under hundred-year-old cedars
anchored firmly to the ground.

HOMESTEAD

It took a while but we finally found
the house my mother grew up in,
moved to a new location but now
unoccupied, a rusted horseshoe
above the front door though missing

the porch where she courted my dad
whose father refused them a loan, saying
"If you're old enough to get married" etc.,
so they borrowed ten bucks to pay the JP
and the rest, as they say, is history.

TAPESTRY

So what do we salvage from memory's
tapestry? A pattern in the linoleum
long since removed for asbestos,
or else the house itself removed
for subsequent urban renewal?

Are the patterns only imagined?
Like your mother and father's
matching reindeer sweaters
they wore only at Christmas,
now moldering in a landfill?

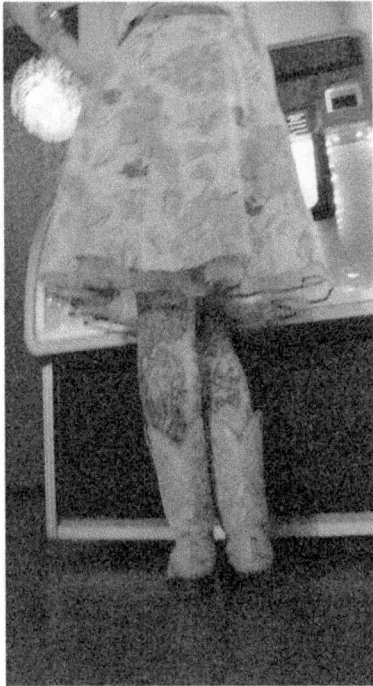

THE PERILS OF CROSS-POLLINATION

If Dad's favorite flower was the daisy,
Mother's was the lowly hollyhock,
otherwise known as "outhouse flower"
because they were planted near privies,
for looks, as nothing could improve the odor.

A common pre-War trick was tipping outhouses
on Halloween, presumably unoccupied.
Which occurs to me now, another October
approaching, the month of my conception,
my parents' seasonal treat, their firstborn.

REMEMBERING DOCTOR JOBE

During my periodic bouts with poison ivy,
I think about the doctor who delivered me,
(a story Mother repeated on every birthday),
who lost his license later for doing abortions.
So when I pay this price for doing yard work,

my blisters weeping like planets giving birth
to their own satellites, I can't help but recall
the most troublesome book in the Bible, God
smiting a true believer on a dare from the Devil,
and count myself lucky it isn't leprosy or boils.

TIT MAN

I've been unable to determine
if we need fewer muscles to smile
than to frown. I was frowning, even
in my baby pictures, due to chronic
constipation, according to Mom,

which she dutifully treated
with Karo Syrup and Pet Milk,
opting not to breast-feed,
thereby inducing a lifelong
fetish of the first magnitude.

NOSTALGIC BRIEF ON CHEATING

On the night shift at the Coffee Shop,
Granny dines out back in the kitchen
with the negroes who work on the KCS.
Elmer Stinnett gives me a buffalo nickel
to stand on the lunch counter and shout

"Call for Philip Morris" as loud as I can,
and the customers laugh because I say
"Silip" instead of "Philip," then laugh even
harder when he sneaks the same coin back
and tricks me to sing the jingle over again.

PHOTO NEGATIVE

I haven't seen a photo negative
in fifty years, another missing
piece to childhood's puzzle,
our family's white faces black,
hair suddenly gone white inside

the confines of the dark-room,
reversals which never occurred
in our respectable small town
where coloreds ate in the kitchen
and took their bitter coffee black.

SEVENTH INNING STRETCH

It was the era when New York City
boasted three Major League teams
and Granny would listen faithfullly
to her beloved Yankees, gloating
over their total domination.

But it was her fondness for cigarettes
that did her in, unfiltered Camels
that rewarded her devotion like
the love she bestowed on baseball,
killing her slowly one cell at a time.

GUN CULTURE: A FOOTNOTE

Our neighbor was a good sport
about getting shot in the leg.
Looking back, I have no idea
what my rookie parents were thinking,
buying a BB-gun for a four-year-old,

or what I was thinking (Mama
working the night-shift, Daddy
away in the war) when I slipped
up on Mr. Allen, suddenly lifted
the barrel and pulled the trigger.

CROW POISON
(for Myrna Ruth)

Singing *Jesus Wants Me for a Sunbeam*
at the Methodist Sunday school.
Killing a stray cat under the woodpile
by siccing the neighbors' dogs,
Bozo and Bear.

Reeder Thornton in the back alley,
exposing himself and making lewd remarks.
The Smittles who lived across the street.
The parsonage nextdoor. Poteau Mountain looming.
The small white flowers blooming in Grandpa's yard.

THE KID HAS AN EAR

There was no piano in our family,
just a fiddle and a battered E-flat tuba
bequeathed by the great-grandfathers.
Therefore my parents' astonishment
when we visited friends with an upright

and I picked out the *Dragnet* theme
first time, including the penultimate
tritone, that most ambivalent interval,
as if I retained the skill from a past life
making me a precocious pre-schooler.

THE SOUND OF ONE LIP BUZZING

When I came home at the age of four
singing Max Steiner's score to John Ford's
She Wore a Yellow Ribbon, my parents
knew I was different. Was there a more
glorious moment in the history of cinema

than the cavalry charging to save the day
with the bugler busting his chops? After a
50-year career as a professional brass player,
I know now that the sound was over-dubbed,
that no one can buzz their lips astride a mare.

UNCONFIRMED RUMORS

Ruby Kelly, whose husband Grady
was full-blood Choctaw and a friend
of my dad, predicted when I was a kid
that my full lips would someday make
a lady happy. She was wrong. Instead

I spent half a century kissing a trombone.
Also she scared me that on Christmas Eve
all the farm animals would bow down
at midnight, dropping on their knees
to commemorate the Baby Jesus.

UP A TREE

I awaken from a dream about acting,
though I haven't acted since first grade
in a church play where I was Zacchaeus,
the tax collector who climbed a tree
to see Jesus, decked out in borrowed

sandals and a Howdy Doody bathrobe,
balanced precariously on a stepladder.
I have long since forgotten my lines
but seem to have spent my life up a tree
waiting for someone to rescue me.

CASE CLOSED

The first day of November in third grade,
I get caught eating Halloween candy
(actually a chunk of orange paraffin).
Mrs. Scott: "Gerry, are you chewing gum?"
Me: "No, mam" (which is partly true).

Mrs. Scott: (to Elsie Walker, the preacher's kid):
"Elsie, what does the Bible say about lying?"
Elsie (piously): "Thou shalt not tell a lie."
I march up front and spit it out, then return
to my desk, my face three shades of red.

OKIE PASSOVER

Back then we were deprived of weather porn.
You know, scare tactics by the networks
to boost their sorry ratings. Instead we
stepped outside and high-tailed it
to the neighbor's storm cellar

if conditions looked suspicious,
huddled nervously with the spiders
among dusty shelves of canned goods.
When the twister warnings lifted, Deelie
always gave us a jar of her famous dill pickles.

LINKS

The petrified wood in Mom's flowerbed
is our remembered linkage to childhood,
and Pete, the green-and-yellow parakeet
who exited one morning on Dad's work hat
then perched on the roof while we pleaded

before he escaped into the Great Unknown.
There was a castor bean by the breezeway
and the black widow underneath a loose
stone, revealed only to select initiates
in our dark version of fraternity.

WE WON IT AT THE MOVIES
(with apologies to Pauline Kael)

We learned more from formula cinema
than we did from church or public schools.
There was little else to do in my hometown,
Dad away in the Navy, Mom not so much
a movie fan as she was keen on winning

the weekly drawing. So our second home
became the Liberty Theater where we saw
the Saturday serials and studio pot-boilers,
and Mother finally won a GE steam-iron
which she used until the cord wore down.

RED ROVER, COME OVER

I suffered chronic nosebleed as a kid,
sometimes for no apparent reason
but usually the result of a flung
limb which sent me to the sidelines.
The town's only physician said I had

"a deviated septum," which Mom
(a trained nurse) would pronounce
proudly, as if it was the password
of a secret society to which I gained
access and she possessed the only key.

LITTLE BIG MAN

An important rite of passage, before
confirmation in the Methodist Church
or owning my first fly-rod and shotgun,
was graduation from the booster seat
to a leather chair at the barber shop,

the same chair occupied by my father
when George Kelly the Choctaw barber
stropped the blade of his straight razor
and carefully scraped it down my neck,
initiating me into the mystery of lather.

BACK STORY

I still have the scar to remind me
of the stupidity of ten-year-olds,
a vague recollection of noting
the high-speed mote one moment
before impact with my left eyebrow.

We never repeated our transgression,
the neighborhood boys who chose
a BB-gun fight at the cemetery,
aware without being told my narrow
escape from blindness was lucky.

NUCLEAR FAMILY (A LULLABY)

Hard to be nostalgic for the 'fifties,
that pot-of-gold at the end of two wars,
strange rainbow that we managed to survive,
apotheosis of white bread and margarine,
of Just Add Hot Water And Serve.

Hard to be nostalgic for the 'fifties,
for the mandated polio vaccine
and Strontium90-laced school milk
before they stopped above-ground testing,
for the duck-and-cover Cold War drills.

CROSS TIES

Though she rarely complained, I wonder
what my young mother was thinking
doing dishes in our house by the tracks,
my baseball pounding the shingles
before rolling off of the roof.

Testing my reflexes or merely bored, I could
never be sure till the ball reappeared.
Compared to the trains which roared by
on schedule, maybe our sounds meant
little in that circumscribed environment.

NAMING NAMES

In eastern Oklahoma everyone had triple names:
Marvin Dale Swaim, Billy Frank Sullivan, Bobby Don Smith,
whose sisters were Janey and Jo Alice (the former
apparently bereft); then there was Paul Albert Riggins,
and Myrna Ruth Kelly, the Choctaw girl who died early

of a ruptured appendix. But I only heard my middle name
when I was in deep trouble, or used by a branch of the family
to distinguish me from an uncle who shared his other name.
But Mother's dad only ever called me "Racehorse," because
I moved so fast and because he had a nickname for everyone.

RAILROAD TOWN

Born between the change from steam to diesel,
I grew up in a railroad town where Mom's family
were railroad men. Andrew Jackson Lynn, named
after his father (named after the Swindler-in-Chief)
worked at the local roundhouse until they went out

on strike and were fired. His son-in-law, my grandpa,
was a strikebreaker, a scab, after which the two men
never spoke, Grandpa Lynn becoming a subsistence
farmer in a Choctaw settlement called Hontubby,
a place where the twenty-dollar-bill was cursed.

KANSAS CITY SOUTHERN

I often thought the KCS
was like a giant centipede,
boxcars bumping rhythmically
like a multi-jointed carapace,
its red caboose for a stinger.

But the elegant Southern Belle
was the embodiment of luxury,
lucky passengers whisked away
to exotic destinations we might
get to see for ourselves someday.

AFTER THE ACCIDENT

Grandpa Irvin was an engineer
for the Kansas City Southern,
later released on disability
because they wouldn't pay
his pension (less than $50/year).

It didn't help when he drove off
and left his train behind one day,
a brakeman flailing frantically
at the next station, assuming
mistakenly that he was waving.

TO THE BUCKEYE IN MY POCKET

Like lovers, you are not the first or last,
disposable when lost or exhausted.
I carry you because my grandpa did,
in the belief that it would ward off
rheumatism and lumbago. I dimly

comprehend the former but don't
have a clue about the latter, erring
as I do on the side of caution,
because you link me to a past
that keeps seeding and receding.

CROSSINGS

Growing up too near the tracks,
I found the sound of trains to be
soothing as well as exciting;
even the midnight freight
proved strangely comforting.

But hermetically-sealed automobiles
forced them to tweak the decibels
so that now the warning signal
is loud enough wake the dead,
if the dead dare be disturbed.

RUNESTONE

Back before there was easy access
our Scout troop trekked up the side
of Poteau Mountain to Kitchen Canyon,
ate our sack lunches under an overhang,
water trickling from a wet-weather spring.

We stretched before ogling the vertical slab
with its eight etched mysterious characters
left behind by Indians or drunken hunters,
though Miss Farley insisted the markings
were the handiwork of early Vikings.

TO THE BOOM TOWNS

We fished or swam in the strip pits
of eastern Oklahoma. Our mothers
tried to frighten us that they were
bottomless, that if we drowned
our bodies would never be found.

Which must have worked because
we quickly transferred to the muddy
rivers and streams, just as the miners
had moved on, their gouged signatures
filling with water like sparkling mirrors.

CAPTIVATED

The summer of our first TV
I could not tear myself away,
my bicycle left outside to rust,
my baseball mitt collecting dust
in the closet, kids looking askance

at my sudden disappearance.
Who could brook comparison
to B-westerns or Perry Mason,
the mindless fare to fog my brain
like Red Skelton and *Wagon Train*?

DEATH OF A TEAMSTER

The last year our neighbor plowed,
I hung out by the fence to hear
this man command an animal
with "gee" or "haw" for right or left
and "whoa" the universal sound for stop,

though he seemed excessively cruel,
incessantly scolding and prodding
like the parent of a headstrong child
swept along on a tide of fossil fuel
and memories of a reluctant mule.

BLOOD LETTING

Seeing Bobby Don Smith's father
slaughter a hog in the back yard –
knocking it out with a sledgehammer
and hanging it up in a tree to bleed –
prepared me for the shower scene

in *Psycho* two years later, sitting there
in the darkened theater with Mother,
watching Janet Leigh's black blood
flow irretrievably down the drain,
turning my universe upside down.

IN THE ABSENCE OF SILKWORMS

Shinnying the fence, I sat on the roof
of the neighbors' toolshed, concealed
by the mitten-shaped leaves
while filling on pilfered mulberries,
my only competition some hungry wrens.

Not that stolen fruit was always sweet.
Sometimes we preferred the tartness
of unripe plums or blackberries,
as if somehow rehearsing for
the often-sour ordeal of adolescence.

LEAVING HEAVENER

It started like one of God's little jokes,
a hick town that spelled out "Heaven,"
my hometown in eastern Oklahoma
on the west side of Poteau Mountain
where the foothills heaved up children.

Then we border-hopped to Arkansas,
a place once called "Hell on the border,"
Fort Smith created to restore the order
between Osage and evicted Cherokees;
from Heaven to Hell at the age of twelve.

III. Ancestry.com

Weep for the crowds of men
Like birds gone south forever

– Gary Snyder

A WARNING

When Franklin dangled a key from his kite
unleashing the force which later became
the central nervous system of the planet,
he could not have foreseen a 3-year-old
in rural Oklahoma inserting a bobby pin

into an electrical outlet and getting
knocked clear across the living room.
But he certainly might have understood
why the child would not need reminding
thenceforth to beware of the unforeseen.

LEFLORE COUNTY IDYLL

Whoever invented childhood innocence
didn't grow up in eastern Oklahoma
where we entertained ourselves
by salting slugs, scorching ants
with a magnifying lens,

or setting Tippy the terrier
on the neighbor's chickens,
Boog Phillips rushing out to shout
"I'll kill that little sonofabitch,"
unclear which one of us he meant.

THE FUTURE OF STANDARDIZED TESTING

Are you walking the dog, or is the dog
walking you? Not everything in life
has easy answers, multiple choice
the worst, where every answer
seems right, though true-and-false

tends to paint the world in black
and white, like a 'fifties photograph.
Look, that's me in the foreground
with a cane pole over my shoulder,
wondering what school will be like.

SUMMERS IN PARADISE

I doubt if the Oklahoma Tire & Supply
sold playground equipment back then,
so Granddad fastened a leftover tire
with a strand of hemp to an oak limb.
It was our hick version of Disneyland

when the cousins would visit in summer
before entertainment became an industry.
When our fathers bothered to swing us,
our stomachs jumped out of our bodies
while the ladies chatted idly in the shade.

KIDDIE PORN

My first glimmerings of sexuality
occurred looking at the lingerie ads
in Granddad's Montgomery Ward catalog,
my favorite model Miss Double-D Lace Bra.
That and seeing Marilyn Monroe undress

in *River of No Return*, hanging her wet
undies out to dry on the nearby bushes.
Add a dash of unadorned gash from Mother's
nursing books, plus that host of titillating
nudes beckoning from the *History of Art*.

ALIEN ODE

Who knows what my elders were thinking
when they came and picked me up to see
Forbidden Planet at the Liberty Theater
back in Heavener, Oklahoma starring
Leslie Nielsen and Walter Pidgeon,

not to mention Robby the Robot
plus an all-electronic music score,
Shakespeare routed to outer space,
my grandparents' frame of reference
only the 'fifties fare on their Zenith TV?

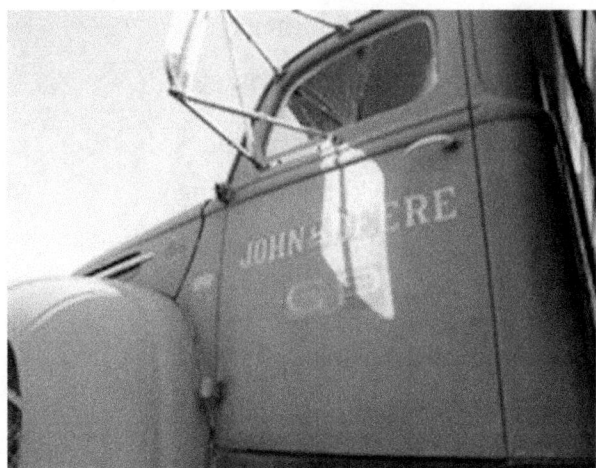

CHAMPAGNE AND SECOND-HAND SMOKE or THE APOTHEOSIS OF KITSCH

Lawrence Welk devised a formula
for his mom-and-pop variety show
those black-and-white decades ago,
magically (or tragically?) transforming
musical style into aural Norman Rockwell.

The soundtrack of their golden years,
it quickened the pulse of our elders
during their Saturday night ritual,
puffing contentedly on a Pall Mall
draped in the vapor consuming us all.

FLASHBACK, 1954

I'm sitting on my grandma's smelly sofa
watching *The Dinah Shore Chevy Show*
and singing along with her sponsor:
"Drive your Chevrolet through the USA,
America's the greatest land of all,"

Uncle Joe just returned from Korea
with shrapnel in his ass, which I only
learned recently, introducing him to
my Chinese relative who almost said
"My grandfather probably shot at you."

OWED TO LOWER LEARNING

Dad taught me how to mimic squirrels
by rubbing the edges of quarters together.
Of course they were made of silver then,
producing a slightly different sound.
He taught me how to aim with my .410.

Granddad taught me how to bait a hook,
to grab a minnow and harden my heart
for the miniature crucifixion, and how
to hold a fish so as not to get finned.
That was my backwoods matriculation.

SCRATCH BISCUITS

In those days Grandma Rose
always had squirrel and dumplings
on the stove, and hot coffee
for the grownups, except
Granddad enjoyed

spooning it out for the kids,
laughing at the faces we made
while our young mothers
faintly protested, afraid
to dispute the ruler on his throne.

IN THE VERNACULAR

He always wore a sweat-stained Stetson
but never any socks. We were struck
by his hairless shins. He was down
to just a single snaggle-tooth but
could go through corn-on-the-cob

like a one-fingered typist and was
even undeterred by fried chicken,
which Rose would catch to wring
its neck then later scald and pluck.
We wondered if he slept in his hat.

NO JOKE

Why did the chicken cross the road?
It isn't gender specific. Maybe another
forlorn hen or the rooster that ran loose
in my granddad's yard and terrified me
as a kid. I often secretly wished him dead.

Maybe it crossed on a dare to escape
the stereotype of being a coward.
Or maybe it was terminally bored,
curious what beckoned over there
on the outskirts of domesticity.

RURAL ELECTRIFICATION COMES TO EASTERN OKLAHOMA

When they dammed the Poteau River
my granddad worked at the power plant
owned by the Lincoln Power Corporation.
They said he returned from work one day
so tired he collapsed on the floor for a nap.

A scorpion fell from the new light fixture
stinging him on the nose, which swelled up
so they said he looked like Reddy Kilowatt
and joked about the episode for decades,
but all he could remember was the pain.

100 PROOF

He pulled all of his teeth with nothing more
than a pair of pliers and some moonshine for
anesthetic. When people inquired how he
stood the pain, he simply said, "It's easy
when they hurt bad enough." Years later,

when I was starting out on trombone,
he would request my rendition of *Taps*
then weep openly, a crusty veteran
who often drew the burial detail,
a memory that whiskey could not kill.

GRANDAD'S WAR

Being older than the green recruits,
it fell his lot to barber the dead
and escort their bodies back home by train,
which beat, hands down, the trenches of Verdun.
Thousands fell without firing a shot

from the 'Spanish flu' at Camp Pike.
He later came back and got married,
waited for the monthly pension check.
That it survived the moths was miraculous,
his trench coat moldering in the smokehouse.

GRANDAD'S FLOWER BEDS
(for the Samuels)

His favorites all started with "p":

petunia, peony, portulaca.

He liked to take the former

and flutter it under my brother's nose,

which would make him shudder then throw up.

Which must have registered somewhere

between strange and downright hilarious

to this trickster with a sadistic streak.

The beds are long gone with their borders of stone,

the homestead now vanished like pollen.

IN PRAISE OF RANDOLPH SCOTT

Granddad never quite recovered
from the surgery for throat cancer
in that generation of smokers, a third
of his neck removed, stomping around
in his Stetson announcing, "The Indians

are coming, hide the women and children."
He wasted away at the VA in Vinita,
delirious and covered with bedsores,
dreaming perhaps of his baseball days
but still missing his last Lucky Strike.

FIRESTARTER

Granddad never missed a chance
for burning off the winter grass,
believing it came back greener in spring.
They say his father died fighting a grassfire,
which may have been family hearsay.

Today their graves are overgrown
with vegetation never kissed by flame,
which now I only visit intermittently,
the non-biodegradable plastic wreaths
their last best chance for immortality.

DAYS OF THEIR LIVES

The examined life is never a cakewalk.
Flop into a chair when the music stops,
the prize a pewter spittoon you will give
to your step-grandmother's mother who
dips while watching *The Days of Our Lives*

on her Philco TV, stuck in the wheelchair
she doesn't need but uses to punish
her husband for imagined infidelity
whenever he flees to the deer camp,
triggering her loss of grip on reality.

SANDWICH

Out of all the things I have forgotten,
why did I choose to remember this?
Is memory even a matter of choice
or does it simply exist, like weather,
or like the hill folk reinventing speech?

I never heard Pop Combs say "I forget."
He only always said "I dis-remember,"
as in "I disremember where you put
the cat food," then made himself
a sandwich mistaking it for hash.

TOUCHED BY GRACE

Uncle Edsel was born subnormal.
Meaning he never learned to read,
though he could distribute the mail
without mistake, maybe memorizing
the script like Koko the talking gorilla.

His teeth eventually rotted away
from the Pepsi salesmen gave him
at the mercantile where he loitered,
cracking jokes in a language all his own
then warming his hands before heading home.

SURPRISE LILIES

The Naked Ladies start their perennial
striptease as the summer slips away.
I doubt if my great-aunt named them,
though she certainly enjoyed repeating
the words, a vestige from Victorian times

when mere assonance could titillate.
Not a leaf in sight, not even the lone
fig-leaf that once covered her *King David*,
pink pinwheel stuck on a long green stalk,
spinning into infinity.

LIMBERDICKS

It's what my father called the old men
in overalls who lived on pension checks
and sat out front of the General Store
telling lies and whittling red-cedar sticks
in his hometown. Forget wood-carving.

That would require some purpose,
and purpose was something they always
shunned while whittling it down to a nub
and spitting tobacco into the dirt before
reaching for a split log to start another.

A CHILD'S CHRISTMAS IN HOWE

It was during the Great Depression, before
recycling was in fashion, that the brothers
(four of them, bereft of sisters) would exchange
homemade newspaper kites on Christmas Eve,
might even receive a real live apple or orange

from their father, or a jar of pear preserves
from Aunt Nellie, the same aunt who, after
their mother died, would herd the naked
boys into the smokehouse on washday
to scrub their only change of overalls.

A WHITE LIE

It was shortly after his mother died.
They had gone out berry-picking
and were coming back in a wagon.
Someone noticed Dad's bucket
was not as full as before

plus the telltale stains on his chin.
"Gerald, are you eating berries again?"
his uncle queried. "No," he replied,
gesticulating towards the sky.
"It wasn't me, it was birds."

NIGHT STALKERS

That you made straight A's is a wonder
as your father couldn't drive and often
kept you out half the night to run
the coon hounds, his main source
of income during the Depression.

What happened after you treed them
is anyone's guess. Your family was not
desperate enough to skin and eat them.
Maybe it's when you acquired the skill
to stalk the Japanese a few years later.

JUST ANOTHER WAR STORY

You weren't allowed to shoot your relatives.
Even in 1940s Oklahoma. Not even the uncle
who stole the ruby ring you gave your dad.
Not even in the butt with birdshot.
So they gave you a choice at 17.

Go to jail or join the Navy. Of course you chose
the latter. Just in time to see the atom bomb
dropped on Hiroshima. For which you lacked
an adequate vocabulary. Settled instead for
silence from which I resurrect your story.

POPEYE THE SAILOR MAN

Never much for war-stories
or tales about the Navy, he
did once mention casually
seeing a large barracuda
cruising in shallow water

snap a beer can in two.
Also mixing grapefruit
juice with alcohol from
dismantled torpedoes.
They called it "joy juice."

A BOUQUET FOR GRANDMA ROSE
(for James Lloyd)

She never swore but for the rare

occasion when we said 'Japan'

and turned the air blue with her epithet

"the goddamn Japs," words joined at the hip

like Siamese triplets because her only son

was killed in combat in the Philippines

and left behind an unborn son

who bore his father's name

because she sneaked it

onto his birth certificate.

BRIEF HISTORY OF THE COLD WAR
(Bikini Atoll, July 1946)

Ironic that a revealing swimsuit was named

for an island we rendered uninhabitable,

sending thousands into exile

"for the good of mankind."

My father, a teenage sailor,

was ordered to crouch on the deck

with his eyes closed. He opened them

to a different world, one in which

his children would wake with nightmares

and school fire-drills would never be the same.

EARTHSPAWN

We didn't know who christened them,
Indians perhaps, the sandstone boulders
randomly dispersed on the hillside above
my granddad's house, sloughed by glaciers
ten thousand years ago, Eagle Eye the largest,

then Eagle Eye's Brother further down,
then Eagle Eye's Cousin, and on and on
in graduated sizes, where we kids would sit
and ponder the nature of relationships,
the wondrous hierarchies of stone and bone.

IV. Father To The Man

The Light in the Eyes

*Who knows
where it goes?*

– Miller Williams

EVERLASTING REGRET

My biggest disappointments
were always interpersonal, Dad
selling my best arrowheads
to the man from Kansas City, Mom
throwing away on moving day

my Mickey Mantle rookie card.
All now would be worth a small
fortune. But it was never about
just the money. More about this
damnable urge to regret the past.

MY BEST YEAR

was the year I played second base
for First Methodist in the church league.
I had good form and could field a ground
ball, and the coaches seemed to like me.
The next year I switched to First Baptist

but was soon replaced at second
by the son of a deacon whose father
happened to be the coach's best friend,
an early lesson in church politics
as my ego reckoned back then.

REFLECTIONS

Commerce has grown so godless
that we pine for Elvis On Velvet,
anyone's secular King of Kings,
or mourn the Fairlane 500
which Dad sold in 1963.

If we could travel back again,
we would listen to him complain
about politics and the price of gas,
nostalgia always providing us
with a tinted looking-glass.

CENTIPEDE

We could not have been more astonished
if Dad's uncle had showed up with a caged
tiger instead of the eight-inch centipede
in a quart fruitjar, threatening with its alien
black body and Halloween-orange legs

that doubled as stingers. Its fate I can't recall –
science-fair project or death in a dumpster –
though now it must suffer the fate of all
the Big Fish stories and Big Snake stories
that vanish on the tongues of the tellers.

TO THE TELLERS

Nobody could tell a story like Dad,
so we sat passively on the sidelines
while he regaled us. After his death,
we ventured forth to reassemble
the mishmash of family history.

Cautious regarding self-censorship,
we strove to find some middle ground
between a bank teller and a truth teller,
an accountant and a keeper of accounts,
hoping to achieve a kind of balance.

OFF COLOR

Dad didn't have much use for literature,
but he liked to sing and had a good ear.
The earliest verses I ever heard were:
"If your pecker's short and your pressure's weak,
step up close or you'll pee on your feet," and

"No matter how you shake and dance,
the last few drops go into your pants."
Ignorant of assonance and alliteration,
he pronounced winters "cold as a witch's tit"
and summers "hotter than the hinges of hell."

"THE F-BOMB"

I never heard my father use that word,
in spite of his otherwise dragon tongue,
the megaton taboo of his generation.
Now commentators routinely allude
to this verbal hurricane downgraded

to a tropical storm, Dad's hydrogen
bomb reduced to a sputtering firecracker.
Movies that curse worst appear in Guinness.
It makes one wonder what we'll use for locks
when nothing's left inside Pandora's box.

SECOND-HAND PTSD

Dad forbade Mom to use the expression
"cooked in their own juices," referring perhaps
to an astronaut mishap. Who knew what
tripwire might trigger his addled brain?
She couldn't even say it in the kitchen,

contextualized by turkey or roast beef.
We only ate our eggs fried over-easy,
which had to be sliced a particular way.
We later learned he toured the scorched
remains of Hiroshima.

LAWS OF COMPENSATION

My father was a math whiz and All-State
basketball star. So I was weak in math
and didn't give a shit about sports.
Punished him instead by becoming
a musician. The annual piano recital.

The band concerts. Him pacing the hall
with a cigarette. Like some caged
animal desperate for an exit. Eager
to be elsewhere. So I married early.
To reassure him I was not a queer.

"THE HORROR"

It wasn't Brando's line in Coppola's movie
but rather a look that crossed my father's face
one night when he was drinking. We argued.
The rest is a blur. Perhaps he was speaking
harshly to my mother and I for once

stood up for her and he drew back his fist
then realized what he was about to do,
released me and suddenly rushed upstairs,
never to speak of the matter again,
but also never again to touch the booze.

ODE TO GOOD INTENTIONS

Dad went through a phase in mid-life
when he challenged my sincerity
on an obligatory greeting card.
I countered with "Sorry, Dad,
they don't make any that say

Happy Birthday, you sonofabitch."
After that he softened considerably
on the saccharine drivel of Hallmark,
reassured I intended what they said
in spite of the rhyme and iambics.

PISSING IN THE YARD

My father remembered chamber pots,
the era preceding indoor plumbing.
In defiance of the porcelain gods,
he said men became too civilized
when they could no longer piss

off their porches. But he was forced
to compromise, relieving himself
in his final years by the fence
behind the garage, our nosy
neighbors too old to care.

PARANOID ODE

They said it was a side effect
of the Parkinson's medication
when he accused his loyal wife
of such a ridiculous indiscretion,
convinced his own granddaughter

had stolen his silver dollar collection,
the boomerang for his lack of trust
consuming him now like the anger
at this disease which forced us
to confiscate his car keys.

7 MEDS

WWII vets were never known as whiners.
When they sent Dad to HealthSouth to rehab,
the nurse said, "Mr. Sloan, on a scale of one
to ten, please rate your pain." "Fifteen,
goddammit," he replied. The night he died,

the hospice nurse asked me to witness
her flushing his seven meds, a hedge
against hillbilly heroin, and I wondered
at the healing arts, if the Arkansas River
was qualified to deal with so much pain.

GONE TO GLORY

"Cain't tell the freckles from the dirt,"
a bluegrass lyric that rhymes with "hurt."
I had my share of both while growing up,
hair so white in summer I was "Cottontop"
to Dad. No church-goer, he loved the songs

heard as a kid at the Hartford sing-alongs,
such as *At the River* and *Amazing Grace*,
plus Brumley's *I'll Fly Away*, of course,
which I softly hum as he slips into a coma,
wayward son of Arkansas and Oklahoma.

CODA

As he dipped gradually into a coma,
I slipped in and put on some music he
would never have consciously chosen,
hoping it might offer a small degree
of solace, the most beautiful music

I know: i.e. the peaceful Adagio
to the Mozart *Clarinet Concerto*,
that it might penetrate somehow
the darker recesses of his brain,
explaining all I could not explain.

STATIONS OF THE CROSS

From a hilltop overlooking Bogotá,
I notice a terrace below covered
with daisies, my father's favorite
flower. Recently deceased, he
might have enjoyed knowing

that the name for daisy in Spanish
is Marguerite, first name of his wife
of sixty years. O Mother, flower
beyond compare, help me to bear
my grief so far from you and Arkansas.

BOX SCORES

Watching customers and reading the paper,
I feel my brain being gradually drained. SUVs
are backed up at the McDonald's drive-thru,
impatient for their coffee and sausage biscuits,
reminding me of his post-retirement klatch

on Saturdays. Shaving in the mirror today, I don't
recognize myself, his face superimposed on mine.
This must have been how my father felt at a time
we weren't getting along, fumbling for something
to say, then rescued once more by the sports page.

AFFIRMATIONS

On a gray and windy day in January,
alone and feeling depressed, sensing
somehow his presence, I speak aloud
to my dead father: "Hello Dad, I know
you're there. I love you and miss you."

Affirmation was never his strong suit;
he withheld it in abundance but makes
up for it today in spades as I glance out
the window to see an untethered silver balloon
announcing just the two words *YOU'RE AMAZING*.

THE BURIAL URN IN MOTHER'S LIVING ROOM

My father's blue-gray eyes reduced to ashes,
the bluebird tattooed on both shoulders,
one for each time he rounded the Cape
of Good Hope. Gone the body hair,
the nails, the freckle on his lower lip.

Gone the uncircumcised cock he rarely
let me see, which stayed permanently
limp after prostate surgery. The skin
and bones still lingering somewhere
in the ozone, now married to the air.

LINES FOR A CHRISTMAS CARD

I have no recollection of this:
my father leaning down to kiss
me on the cheek one Christmas,
depicted in an old photograph
my mother recently shared.

Instead I chose to remember
the hurt instead of the happiness,
which could almost be forgiven
after the incomparable gift
of teaching me to fly-fish.

FINDING TRUE NORTH

In my early teens Dad tried to teach me
the rudiments of hunting, to observe
how if I lost my bearings in the woods
lichen grew on the north side of trees
and how to lead a bird or mammal

based on size and estimated speed.
Walking in the park today with Mother,
I point out how the north wall is splotched
with lichen, while the south wall is mostly
bare as my father's ten-year vacancy.

HARMONIUM

was the pump-organ Dad rescued from a barn
in a backwater somewhere south of Fort Smith,
caked with a decades-old veneer of chicken shit.
But the pedal still worked. Also, surprisingly, all
of the reeds. He probably paid a hundred bucks

but could easily have gotten a couple of grand
after restoration, much sanding and refinishing.
Instead it became an heirloom where someone
could thrash out a Bach chorale, or given the right
request might retrieve a hymn or Christmas carol.

MEMORIAL DAY, 2017

Hi, Dad. Great catching up with you today
in the video interview by
the historical society,
their archive for survivors of WWII.
You were handsome even in your decline.

That you posed in your beaver-skin cap
is indicative, always out-of-step
with the times, a throwback
like the mountain men
who stole this land from the Indians.

V. Epilogue: Hitchhiking To Eternity

Face to face again against
The unfolding unforeseen

– John Rule

B-POSITIVE

I sometimes wonder if it's just another
of God's little wink-wink jokes, advising me
through blood type to adjust my attitude.
Rarely did I smile in childhood photos.
Had I paid closer attention in Biology

I might better unravel the mystery
of how O-negative parents could sire
such a freak of nature, at odds with God's
plan that His children be happy (dammit)
whenever I cut my finger or give blood.

LUCK OF THE DRAW

Whenever my thumb starts to quiver
(Dad's early warning for Parkinson's),
I worry it may be sneaking up on me.
And if there's retention when I pee,
I wonder if his prostate cancer

is recycling, and if future infirmity
is just a matter of luck or whether
it's programmed into our genes.
We all must muster the courage
to learn what suffering means.

CORNBREAD EPISTIMOLOGY

It's one of the few things I have mastered
because of who I am and where I'm from
and understand it isn't a pastry
let alone the texture of angel food,
rather something coarse and common

with a mouthfeel always a bit gritty.
Don't dare use a butter substitute.
If we all must die of something,
better to die of scratch cornbread
served hot with a dollop of molasses.

HOMECOMING

Thomas Wolfe got it partly wrong.
You can go home again, up to a point,
in early adulthood. But if you live long
enough things start to change irrevocably,
mostly growing smaller and more rundown

then eventually disappearing altogether, so
that you will become the old codger who
will go there with your grandchildren
and point to the vacant lot, saying,
"Grandpa used to live right here."

BEAUTIFUL DREAMERS

Be careful what you dream for your children
and grandchildren. My granddad would say
"Maybe Gerry will get good enough to play
with Lawrence Welk someday." Sure enough,
years later, after they were put out to pasture

in Branson, MO, their bass trombonist broke his leg
and I was summoned one week to sub, two shows
per day, escorting Peggy Lennon across the stage
in Victorian caroler attire, then grabbing my horn
for the overture, Granddad smiling somewhere.

TOUCHDOWN

My last and favorite uncle passed
away at 11:00am Pacific Time, had
roused up in the night to announce,
"Well, today is the day!" his daughter
believing him to be delirious, although

in the annals of Famous Last Words
his rival W. C. Fields' apocryphal wish
to be in Philadelphia: Joe Bert Irvin,
probably in a Heavener Wolves uniform,
running for his one and only touchdown.

LOW-HANGING CLOUDS

We once made fun of Mother for asking
"Is it fog or just a low-hanging cloud?"
Which seems like a legitimate question
in retrospect, but anything she said
was subject instantly to ridicule.

We wake today to impaired visibility,
and I'm tempted to repeat her query
decades later, because we live on a hill
and because the sun will come out later
melting our family history like vapor.

SISTERS

She might have taken too much laudanum,
the neighbor who swore two white doves
flew out the window the day they died –
Martha Lou and Mary Sue – the twins.
Whether real or imagined, her story

helped the family deal with tragedy.
Buried in the cemetery south of town,
they sleep now side by side, just as they
once lived, their shared headstone like
their too brief lives, never to be repeated.

BREAKING BREAD
(Susan Lynn Irvin, 1903–1972)

My bow-legged Cherokee grandmother
was born in Indian Territory
and rode a horse ten miles to school.
She finished the eighth grade,
married at eighteen, had seven kids,

left her abusive husband at fifty-one.
Tomorrow I will make her recipe
for bean bread, scatter crumbs to the six
directions in honor of her bravery,
hitchhiking to eternity in a wheelchair.

MISSING THE DEAD

My mother's mother moved in with us
after a stroke left her partially paralyzed.
Confined to a wheelchair, she would get
misty-eyed when I put on my Joan Baez LP
singing, "All my trials, Lord, soon be over."

Decades later, especially during the holidays,
I think about the dead and what they endured,
how they continue to touch our lives in ways
we don't fully understand, how they can be
simultaneously with-us yet so not-with-us.

NOTES

ANCESTRAL ODE. This was the only generation that spelled our family name Slone instead of Sloan (Scotch-Irish), possibly phonetic if they were illiterate. Dad said he remembered it spelled that way on their mailbox. Family lore said her husband, Redmond Slone, was killed by bushwhackers in 1862. Later information claims "he disappeared between his house and barn," his body never found. My theory is that he was abducted by one of the conscription bands which roamed the region recruiting for the Confederate Army. They would often give you an ultimatum at gunpoint. At any rate, he left his wife alone to rear five small children. This occurred in Crawford county, Arkansas, several miles east of the town of Rudy.

THE LORD'S WORK. Paraphrase of a folktale collected by Vance Randolph, the preeminent preserver of Ozark folklore.

OSAGE ORANGE. Otherwise known as *bois d'arc*, the French meaning "wood for bows," early explorers noting trees the Osage Indians used for making bows and arrows. We used to call them horse-apples because of the sticky green fruit inedible except by squirrels (the seeds, after the fruit dried out). Rick Squires gave me a set of coasters he made from this wood. This is an update from my previous collection *Paper Lanterns*.

CROW POISON. Wildflower also known as false garlic. Cherokee legend tells that they would use this plant to make a poison that would kill the crows eating their corn.

WE WON IT AT THE MOVIES. Pauline Kael was longtime film reviewer for *The New Yorker*, author of a collection called *We Lost It at the Movies*.

NAMING NAMES. Not-so-veiled allusion to the House UnAmerican Activities Committee which launched a witch hunt against suspected "Communists" in the 1950s and destroyed many careers of people in the arts, especially in Hollywood.

RAILROAD TOWN. Two generations of my mother's ancestors were named after Andrew Jackson, the President who presided over the infamous "Indian Removal" of the 1830s, when the Five Civilized Tribes were uprooted and relocated to Indian Territory, what later became the state of Oklahoma. Jackson's picture on the twenty-dollar-bill was much reviled by their descendants.

RUNESTONE. Gloria Farley ("Miss Farley" to us, though she was married) was my Sunday school teacher at age four. She later authored the book *In Plain Sight: Old World Records in Ancient America* (1994) which attributed the Heavener runestone to early Vikings. Dr. Lee W. Woodard published a counter-narrative (*'7 Noms' at Wicked Fork Where La Salle Died*) which argued that the runes were left by a ragtag group of Frenchmen in 1687 following the murder of their leader on the Fourche Maline, a tributary of the Poteau River now at the bottom of Wister Lake. It reads like a cliffhanger mystery but seems more plausible than the Viking theory. They used runes to avoid detection by Spanish soldiers who owned and patrolled the region. The runestone was a state park before being de-funded.

LITTLE BIG MAN: Cribbing the title of Arthur Penn's 1970 movie starring Dustin Hoffman.

LEAVING HEAVENER. Pronounced "HEEV-ner," a small town in eastern Oklahoma known chiefly for the landmark noted above and named after Joe Heavener, an early settler. My father designed a belt buckle for the Heavener centennial (1896–1996). See page 143.

ALIEN ODE. "Shakespeare routed" refers to the movie's being loosely based on *The Tempest.* The ground-breaking electronic score was composed by Louis and Bebe Barron.

GRANDDAD'S FLOWER BEDS. Dedication to my grandfather and brother: Samuel Layton Sloan and Samuel Stephen Sloan, respectively

IN PRAISE OF RANDOLPH SCOTT. Star of many B-westerns and my grandfather's favorite actor. The disclosure that Scott (the archetypal tough guy) was gay would probably make Granddad squirm in his grave.

SURPRISE LILIES. *King David* refers to a cheap reproduction of Michelangelo's famous sculpture *David,* though the original had no fig-leaf, our puritanical overseers always on the lookout.

A CHILD'S CHRISTMAS IN HOWE. That's Howe, Oklahoma, my father's hometown, a hamlet just north of Heavener, my mother's hometown. Oblique reference to Dylan Thomas's memoir *A Child's Christmas in Wales.*

BRIEF HISTORY OF THE COLD WAR. Ironically, the refugees from the Marshall Islands were relocated in Springdale, Arkansas, after we rendered their homeland uninhabitable. A further irony: the U.S.S. Arkansas was one of the dozen ships expended for our hydrogen bomb test at Bikini Atoll!

GONE TO GLORY. A reference here to the A. O. Brumley sing-alongs in Hartford, Arkansas which my father attended as a child and fondly remembered. Now the obituaries all say "died" or "passed away." "Gone to Glory" is a folksier out-of-date euphemism.

BEAUTIFUL DREAMERS. Stephen Foster's *Beautiful Dreamer* was my grandfather's favorite song. One of my operating aphorisms has always been: Be careful what you wish because you will probably get it! Peggy Lennon was one of the famous Lennon Sisters who had performed with Welk since childhood.

BREAKING BREAD. My grandmother went to her grave convinced she was Cherokee, though it doesn't show in our DNA. Indeed she would turn dark brown in summer. Two of her prized possessions were her Cherokee cookbooks, now in my possession. Actually, her ancestors might have been Keetoowahs, the Old Settlers who came here prior to Indian Removal. I will allow her the benefit of the doubt.

BIOGRAPHIES

GERRY SLOAN was born in Oklahoma City on July 20, 1947 and moved shortly thereafter to Heavener. Judging from the picture above, taken in front of his grandpa's house at age 3, he has spent his life "leaving Heavener." When Gerry retired four years ago from a lifelong career in music, he began creating this cycle of poems based on his early childhood. The poems are interspersed with photographs by Gerry's friend Rick Squires, not to "illustrate" the poetry but to create a parallel gallery evoking similar imagery. Rick was diagnosed several years ago with early onset Parkinson's Disease, which mirrors the experience of Gerry's father depicted in some of the poems.

RICK SQUIRES was born in Stuttgart, Germany and now lives in Fayetteville, Arkansas. He earned a degree in engineering from the University of Oklahoma, worked in the construction business, is the father of four children, was diagnosed with Parkinson's Disease at age 35, took up woodworking and songwriting, released a CD of his songs in 2016 with Danish singer/ composer/ guitarist Grith Böcher (see *MindSigh*), and spends the rest of his time photographing the rural Ozarks.

INDEX OF TITLES

www.ingramcontent.com/pod-product-compliance
Lightning Source LLC
LaVergne TN
LVHW021458080426
835509LV00018B/2326